DATE DUE		

THE JOHN BROWN SLAVERY REVOLT TRIAL

A Headline Court Case

David DeVillers

Enslow Publishers, Inc.

40 Industrial Road   PO Box 38
Box 398   Aldershot
Berkeley Heights, NJ 07922   Hants GU12 6BP
USA   UK

http://www.enslow.com

The author wishes to thank his wife, Julie DeVillers; the United States Department of the Interior; the National Park Service; and the Harpers Ferry Historical Park.

Library of Congress Cataloging-in-Publication Data

DeVillers, David.
    The John Brown slavery revolt trial: a headline court case / David DeVillers.
        p. cm. — (Headline court cases)
        Includes bibliographical references and index.
    Summary: Focuses on the trial of the abolitionist who was hanged for treason and murder following his attempt to capture a military arsenal and arm the slaves for revolt.
    ISBN 0-7660-1385-5
    1. Brown, John, 1800–1859—Trials, litigation, etc—Juvenile literature. 2. Trials (Treason)—West Virginia—Charles Town—Juvenile literature. 3. Harpers Ferry (W. Va.)—History—John Brown's Raid, 1859— Juvenile literature. 4. Antislavery movements—United States—Juvenile literature. [1. Brown, John, 1800–1859—Trials, litigation, etc. 2. Trials (Treason) 3. Trials (Murder) 4. Abolitionists. 5. Antislavery movements.] I. Title II. Series.
    KF223.B76548   2000
    306.3'62'0975499—dc21   99-40386
                                                CIP

Photo Credits: National Archives, p. 1; National Park Service/Harpers Ferry National Historical Park, pp. 6, 11, 15, 23, 26, 32, 35, 43, 50, 57, 66, 71, 76, 86, 90.

Cover Photo: National Archives

Contents

Headline Court Cases

The Andersonville Prison Civil War Crimes Trial
A Headline Court Case
0-7660-1386-3

The John Brown Slavery Revolt Trial
A Headline Court Case
0-7660-1385-5

The Lindbergh Baby Kidnapping Trial
A Headline Court Case
0-7660-1389-8

The Lizzie Borden "Axe Murder" Trial
A Headline Court Case
0-7660-1422-3

The Nuremberg Nazi War Crimes Trial
A Headline Court Case
0-7660-1384-7

The Sacco and Vanzetti Controversial Murder Trial
A Headline Court Case
0-7660-1387-1

The Salem Witchcraft Trials
A Headline Court Case
0-7660-1383-9

The Scopes Monkey Trial
A Headline Court Case
0-7660-1388-X

chapter one

A NATION DIVIDED

CIVIL WAR—In 1859 the United States found itself on the brink of what would be the bloodiest war in its history. The war would not be fought with a foreign power but rather between two parts of the United States. The American Civil War began in 1861 and ended in 1865. More Americans died in the Civil War than in any other war before or after. What could bring a nation to war with itself? Although there were many social and political reasons for the Civil War, the single most significant issue dividing the nation was slavery.

In the fall of 1859 the nation was divided in its opinions on slavery. In the North, where slavery had been illegal for decades, more and more people wanted to end slavery in its entirety. Still more people wanted at least to end the expansion of slavery into the new states. In the South, slavery was a way of life. It was deeply rooted in the culture of the region and the economy. Southerners resented what they felt was Northern interference with their way of life.

Hoping to start a slave rebellion, John Brown attacked a federal armory in the small Virginia town of Harpers Ferry. This picture was taken before the attack.

John Brown was an abolitionist. As an abolitionist, he wanted an end to slavery in all states. Brown felt it was his moral and religious duty to end slavery at any cost—including bloodshed.[1] He acted on his beliefs in the small Virginia town of Harpers Ferry in 1859.

In the hope of starting a slave rebellion, Brown and a handful of loyal followers attacked a federal armory, the building where weapons and ammunition were stored in the small town. The doomed plan was to seize the weapons at the armory and arm the hundreds of slaves who would flock to Harpers Ferry. The plan failed miserably.

The trial, however, captured the attention of the ever-dividing nation. Because Brown's attack took place within the state of Virginia and did not violate any federal laws, the trial would be held in Virginia, before a state, rather than a federal, court. In the South, Virginia was seen as a powerful leader of the Southern way of life. In the North, Virginia was seen as a powerful leader of the evil institution of slavery. If convicted, Brown could be executed, thus creating an abolitionist martyr (one who dies for a cause). Others would see the sacrifice Brown had made and join the abolitionist movement. If the North interfered with the trial or made a rescue attempt, the South would surely respond with violence against the North.

The South would attempt to put the abolitionist movement and the North on trial. John Brown would attempt to put slavery and the South on trial. No trial in the history of the United States would change more people's lives.

chapter two

THE INSTITUTION OF SLAVERY

AMERICA—Slavery was a heavily debated topic even before the United States had gained its independence from England in 1776. The slave trade involved the forced removal of slaves from Africa and their transfer to the United States. The practice of slavery began in Colonial America in the 1600s. It flourished on the South's large plantations, where a large part of the world's supply of cotton and tobacco were grown. In order to be profitable, these plantations needed many workers to serve as cheap labor. Slavery seemed to be the answer to the South's labor needs. In the North, where industries and small family farms were most common, slavery was less profitable and thus rare.

During the time of the Revolutionary War (1775–1783), many Americans began to view slavery as unjust and inhumane. Religious leaders, mostly in the North, began to condemn slavery as violating God's law. With the Declaration of Independence and the spirit of liberty that fueled the

Revolutionary War, many Americans thought it was hypocritical to continue to allow the existence of slavery. Thomas Jefferson, a Southerner who wrote the Declaration of Independence, spoke out against slavery. Jefferson was a good example of the realities of slavery in the South. Although morally opposed to it, he owned slaves and needed them to make his plantation at Monticello profitable.

From the Revolutionary War to the Civil War in 1861, slavery remained strong in the South. Only about one fourth of all white people in the South owned slaves, but the slave owners had political and economic power. Many Southerners believed that their economy would collapse without slavery. Slavery had become so entwined in the Southern way of life that any attempt to end it was seen as an attempt to end the South.

As support for slavery solidified in the South, opposition to slavery grew in the North. Most Northerners felt that slavery would eventually end in a peaceful matter, through state laws or a constitutional amendment, as was done in other countries. For example, one of the single most powerful influences strengthening the antislavery movement was the decision of Great Britain to end slavery in all of its holdings. For the time being, most Northerners were content to see slavery confined to the South and not spread to the new territories in the West. Still, a growing minority of Northerners wanted to end slavery in its entirety.

Quakers, a religious group based in Pennsylvania, had long despised slavery and had set up the Underground Railroad to help fugitive slaves escape to Canada, where they would be safe. The Underground Railroad was not a real railroad; instead, it was a system of safe houses in the North that would protect runaway slaves. The Fugitive Slave Act of 1793 was a federal law that applied to both Northern and Southern states. The law required runaway slaves to be returned to their owners. This law was unpopular in the North, and the Underground Railroad, although illegal, helped free thousands of slaves.

Abolitionist was the term used to describe anyone who wanted to end slavery throughout the country. The abolitionist movement gained momentum in 1816 with the creation of the American Colonization Society. The society protested against slavery and against sending freed slaves to Liberia in East Africa.

As the movement grew, newspapers and other publications devoted to ending slavery sprang up in the North. Some of these papers were seen as radical and extreme. Some papers supported only a peaceful end to slavery, but others demanded an immediate end at any cost. In reaction to these papers, some supporters of slavery threatened and even murdered the publishers. Despite this, newspapers such as William Lloyd Garrison's *The Liberator* in Boston, Massachusetts, thrived and converted more people to the abolitionist cause.

Even as the Northern opinion was turning more and more against slavery, there was a political balance that, at least temporarily, kept the North and the South from any serious clash over the issue. A series of political

Franklin B. Sanborn was one of the Northern abolitionists who supported John Brown.

compromises protected this delicate balance. The first was the Missouri Compromise.

Missouri Compromise

In 1818 there were eleven slave states and eleven free states. Because each state had two senators representing it, this meant that there were twenty-two proslavery senators and twenty-two antislavery senators in the Senate. No federal law can pass without the majority of the Senate voting for it. Thus, neither side had a majority to pass either proslavery or antislavery federal laws. In 1818 the Missouri Territory had applied to become a state. The territory was part of the larger Louisiana Purchase, which lay just west of the states that had already been admitted to the Union. Slavery was legal in that territory, and it already had thousands of slaves in it. If Missouri was admitted as a slave state, it would disturb the political balance.

After heated debate in Congress, a compromise was met. Missouri would be admitted as a slave state, but Maine, another new state in the Northeast, would be admitted as a free state. An imaginary line was drawn through the rest of the Louisiana Purchase. Anything north of the southern border of Missouri (except for Missouri itself) would be free territory, and anything south would be slave territory. The compromise would stand for the next thirty-four years.

Nat Turner

In 1831 terror struck the South in the form of a preacher slave named Nat Turner. Turner was a slave in Virginia who taught himself to read and write (despite the fact that slave owners forbade it). He became a preacher and a leader in the slave community. Turner believed that God wanted him to lead the slaves out of bondage.[1] He acted on this belief and led the bloodiest and most successful slave rebellion in United States history.

Turner, with only a handful of slaves, started the rebellion on August 22, 1831, by killing his owner, Joseph Travis. Turner and the others started with only hatchets but soon gathered muskets and recruited more rebel slaves. Some slave recruits did not volunteer, however; a number of slaves were threatened and forced to aid in the rebellion. The rebellion was so swift that the Virginia militia did not have time to react until great damage was done. The rebellion only lasted three days, but Turner was able to gather over sixty slaves who killed about sixty white people. Turner was not captured until October 30. He and about twenty of the rebelling slaves were hanged for their actions.

Nat Turner's rebellion created a sense of fear in the South that would not end for decades. The South's immediate reaction to the rebellion resulted in the deaths of about one hundred innocent slaves. To ensure that such a rebellion could not be repeated, many Southern states passed laws restricting the education of slaves and the speech of slave preachers. Other Southern states went so far as to pass laws prohibiting both blacks and whites from criticizing slavery.

Many Southerners blamed the North for the rebellion. William Lloyd Garrison's abolitionist newspaper had started only months before the rebellion. In *The Liberator*, Garrison called for the immediate end to slavery. Despite the fact that Nat Turner had probably never even heard of *The Liberator*, many Southerners pointed to Garrison and other abolitionists as the cause of Turner's rebellion. Southern post offices began to confiscate abolitionist literature.

In the North, Turner's rebellion strengthened the abolitionist cause. Many Northerners now felt that the only way to end future bloodshed was to end slavery.

The South took the complete opposite approach by tightening its grip on slavery, making it even more oppressive then ever. Instead of viewing Turner's rebellion as the desperate attempt of an enslaved man to free his people, the South saw itself as the victim of the Northern influences. Historian Steven B. Oates described the next two decades as a period

> during which the South, threatened it seemed by internal and external enemies, became a closed, martial society determined to preserve its slave-based civilization at whatever cost. If southerners had once apologized for slavery as a necessary evil, they now trumpeted that institution as a positive good.[2]

The South would be safe from the threat of slave rebellion for the next twenty-eight years. The next threat would also be from a preacher who believed that God meant for him to free the slaves. But this time the threat would come from a white man from the North.

The abolitionist movement gained momentum in the 1830s and 1840s. Both men and women joined the movement, creating groups and giving speeches. Free blacks such as wealthy James Forten and Robert Purvis played a large role in the movement as well. One of the most famous and influential black men of the time was Frederick Douglass.

Frederick Douglass

Frederick Douglass was born a slave in the Southern state of Maryland. His name was actually Frederick Augustus Washington Bailey. In 1838 he fled his master, went to the

This painting of John Brown portrays his passion for abolition.

free state of Massachusetts, and changed his name to Frederick Douglass. (Many slaves who had been forced to adopt the names of their masters changed their names once they were free.) The self-educated Douglass was a great speaker, and the Massachusetts Anti-Slavery Society soon hired him to speak. In 1845 he wrote his autobiography, *Narrative of the Life of Frederick Douglass.* Soon after the book was published, Douglass fled to England in fear of being arrested and returned to his master. In England, he continued lecturing and raising money to purchase his freedom.

In 1846 Douglass purchased his freedom and returned to the United States. In 1847 he started the abolitionist paper *The North Star,* based in Rochester, New York. He enraged Southerners and influenced thousands of Northerners. Douglass, like many abolitionists, wanted to end slavery through political means. One of the Northerners whom Douglass influenced was a radical abolitionist named John Brown. Brown meant to end slavery through an entirely different means.[3]

Political Parties to End Slavery

In the 1840s the political means to end slavery became at least a possibility. The Liberty party, formed by abolitionists, would propose candidates for office. The Democratic party and the Whig party dominated politics at the time, but the Liberty party candidates won some local elections and had some unsuccessful presidential candidates. The Liberty party also brought slavery to the forefront of politics and forced the other party candidates to take a stance on the issue.

In 1848 the Free Soil party was formed to stop the spread of slavery into the new territories. By 1854 most of the Whig, Free Soil, and Liberty parties, in effect, merged to form the Republican party. The Republican party had a large platform of many different issues. The South correctly saw the Republican party as a real threat to the institution of slavery.

Harriet Beecher Stowe and *Uncle Tom's Cabin*

One of the greatest threats to the institution of slavery was not a radical revolutionary or a political party—it was a book written by a white woman. In 1851 Harriet Beecher Stowe's novel *Uncle Tom's Cabin* was published. The book depicted the harsh, cruel life of a slave in the South. Many Southerners denounced the book as a lie. Northerners, however, praised the book like perhaps no other book in the history of the United States. It sold millions of copies and further divided the people of the North and the South.

The Kansas-Nebraska Act

In the first half of the 1800s numerous compromises by the federal government, such as the Missouri Compromise, were able to keep bloodshed over slavery to a minimum. In 1854 a law passed by Congress, again intended to be a peaceful compromise, failed.

Like Missouri before it, the territories of Kansas and Nebraska were now petitioning Congress to become states. The Missouri Compromise stated that all new states north of

Missouri's southern border, except Missouri itself, would be free states. Both Kansas and Nebraska were north of that border. The South, fearing that two new free states would tip the balance in the Senate, opposed their entrance into the Union.

In 1854 the Kansas-Nebraska Act was passed by Congress. This act provided that new states would not automatically become free states. Instead, citizens of each state would vote to decide the issue. The act made the Missouri Compromise void and made slavery legally possible in what many considered Northern territory. Many Northerners were outraged.

The race was now on for slavery supporters and opponents to get to the new territories, settle there, and vote in support of their side. The result would be the conflict known as Bleeding Kansas, the first direct bloodshed between the North and the South. The most infamous leader to come out of Bleeding Kansas was a fearless and tenacious abolitionist named John Brown.

chapter three

JOHN BROWN: THE MAN

NEW ENGLAND—John Brown was born in Torrington, Connecticut, on May 9, 1800. His parents were Owen and Ruth Mills Brown. Owen Brown was a religious man who actively opposed slavery. He worked with the Underground Railroad, helping to send fugitive slaves to Canada. The family was not considered wealthy, but they were not poor, either. Owen made a living as a farmer, a shoemaker, and a tanner (a person who treats animal hides for leather).

When John Brown was five, he and his parents moved west to Hudson, Ohio. John received his education there and grew up a hardworking and religious young man. His father taught him that slavery was against God's will. At the age of sixteen he moved from Ohio with his brother to Massachusetts to enter the ministry. At the time, Massachusetts was a center for the abolitionist movement, especially in the ministry. As a result of health problems and a lack of money, John was forced to return to Ohio after only a couple of years. He brought back with him an even stronger opposition to slavery.

In Ohio, John worked at his father's tannery (a place where animal hides are treated for leather), and at the age of twenty-two he married Dianthe Lusk. They would eventually have seven children together, but only two would live to adulthood. Around 1826 Brown and his family moved to Randolph, Pennsylvania. Brown found business success there. He built and operated his own tannery, and it was very profitable.

In 1832 Brown's wife died during childbirth. A year later Brown married his second wife, Mary Ann Day. They had thirteen children together, but only six of them lived to adulthood. Brown began to invest in real estate, and by 1837 he had most of his money tied up in these investments. That same year a depression, or major economic downturn, hit the American economy. The result was economically devastating, and by 1842, Brown was bankrupt.

With all his money gone, Brown started over. He moved back to Ohio and managed a large flock of sheep for wealthy businessman Simon Perkins. In 1846 he moved to Springfield, Massachusetts, where he was placed in charge of a wool depot opened by Perkins to sell his wool in the East.

In Massachusetts, Brown began to get involved in the abolitionist cause. He spoke to anyone who would listen to him about the evils of slavery. He wrote articles condemning slavery in abolitionist newspapers. Brown was enraged by the Fugitive Slave Act, which required that runaway slaves be captured and returned to their Southern owners. In 1851 Brown began to organize free blacks in Springfield to resist the law. Brown had become a well-known abolitionist who was not afraid of violating federal law to further the abolitionist cause.

Exactly how far was Brown willing to go to end slavery? In 1847 abolitionist and freed slave Frederick Douglass learned the answer to that question. Brown invited Douglass to his house in Springfield to meet and discuss the direction of the abolitionist movement. Later Douglass would write about the famous meeting and Brown's position on how to end slavery:

> He [Brown] denounced slavery in look and language fierce and bitter; thought that slaveholders had forfeited their right to live; that the slaves had the right to gain their liberty in any way they could; did not believe that moral suasion [influence or persuasion] would ever liberate the slave or that political action would ever abolish the system.[1]

Like Nat Turner before him, John Brown felt that the only way to end slavery was through violent revolution. He felt that he had the moral right to kill slave owners and supporters of slavery for the purpose of ending slavery. He had no confidence that the nation as a whole would ever end slavery on its own.

Frederick Douglass thought John Brown's plan was impractical. He felt that the South would crush any large-scale slave revolt. Douglass knew that only a national force could put a lasting end to slavery. Douglass was not morally opposed to a violent means to end slavery—indeed, he was an important supporter of the upcoming Civil War—he merely felt that Brown's plan was doomed to failure.[2]

Douglass was, nevertheless, impressed with John Brown, the man. At their meeting Douglass observed the John Brown that the rest of the country would soon come to know. Douglass would later write of John Brown:

> Whenever he spoke his words commanded earnest attention. His arguments, which I ventured at some points to oppose, seemed to convince all. Certainly I never felt myself in the presence of a stronger religious influence than while in this man's house.[3]

John Brown's Plan

It would be a number of years before John Brown would put his plan into action. He first needed financial backing from wealthy abolitionists. One such abolitionist was Gerrit Smith. Smith donated 120,000 acres of land in North Elba, New York, for the settlement of free Northern blacks. In 1849 Brown bought 224 of those acres of land and moved to North Elba to assist the settlement. After moving back and forth from Akron, Ohio, and North Elba, John Brown finished his obligations with Simon Perkins. By 1854 he was able to concentrate fully on his financing and preparing for the slave rebellion.

In that same year, events in the West would postpone John Brown's plan. The Kansas-Nebraska Act was passed in May 1854. The act provided that the people of those territories would vote to decide whether new states would be admitted as slave states or as free states. Both Northern free-state supporters and Southern slavery supporters poured money and men into the territories. Three of John Brown's sons, Owen, Frederick, and Saloman, joined the free-state supporters. In spring 1855 they and their families settled near Osawatomie, Kansas.

In 1832, Brown's first wife died during childbirth. A year later Brown married Mary Ann Day, shown here with him in his jail cell during the trial that followed his raid.

When John Brown's sons moved to Kansas, they found a territory engulfed in terror. Proslavery Missourians would often invade the territory, attacking free-state men and destroying their homes. At election time, Missourians crossed the border, threatened free-state voters, illegally voted for proslavery candidates, and went home. Murders were common, and Kansas soon became known as Bleeding Kansas. Soon proslavery men dominated Kansas government. Laws were passed legalizing slavery and making it a crime for people to even protest against it.

When John Brown received word of the plight of his sons and the other free-state residents, he made plans to move to Kansas to fight the slavery supporters. In 1855, armed with weapons paid for by Northern abolitionists, Brown moved to Kansas. He then helped organize a militia to protect the free-state residents of Osawatomie. Outnumbered and possessing inferior weapons, Brown planned to employ guerrilla warfare, or hit-and-run tactics, against the proslavery forces. Because Brown would certainly lose a fight taking on all of the proslavery forces at once, his plan was to use his small force to attack and then disengage before the enemy could counterattack.

On May 22, 1855, John Brown, his sons, and others from the Osawatomie area marched toward Lawrence, Kansas. Lawrence was a town in a free state, and it was under threat of attack from proslavery forces. With the recent murder of two free-state men, Brown and his men were already outraged by the acts of the proslavery men. Before they reached Lawrence, they learned that they were too late. Four hundred proslavery men had taken a number of free-state men as prisoners and burned a hotel and a free-state leader's house. They also destroyed the presses of two free-state newspapers.

John Brown was outraged. He no longer wanted to merely defend free-state settlements; he wanted to go on the offensive. He thought it was time to "fight fire with fire," to "strike terror in the hearts of the pro-slavery people."[4] He said "it was better that a score of bad men should die than that one man who came here to make Kansas a Free State should be driven out."[5] His plan was to go through the Pottawatomie Creek area to seek out and kill proslavery leaders responsible for the recent attacks on the free-state settlements. Members of his party were reluctant to carry out Brown's plan. But as Brown would demonstrate time and time again, his words and personality would convince the men to follow him.

The next evening John Brown and his men approached the cabin of proslavery leader William Doyle. Brown knocked on the door. When Doyle answered, Brown and his men rushed in the house and demanded that Doyle and his two sons surrender to them. Doyle's wife, sensing what was about to come, begged Brown not to take her youngest son who was fourteen. Brown agreed but did take Drury Doyle, age twenty. Brown took the men about a hundred yards down the road, where his men hacked them to death with broad swords.

The first blood of that evening had been spilled. In the end, five proslavery men were dragged from their homes and killed. Although John Brown himself never actually struck a blow to kill any of the men, they were all killed on his orders. Brown's war on slavery had begun and would not end for another four years.

Following the killings, Brown and his men went into hiding. Opinion on the killings varied. Whereas some Northerners were disgusted by what John Brown had done, others saw him as a hero of the abolitionist cause. In the South, newspapers condemned Brown as a Northern monster and ignored the violent acts of the proslavery forces.

John Brown did not hide for long, however. In June 1855 he defeated and captured a force of twenty-three proslavery

Four years before the raid on Harpers Ferry shown here, John Brown fought to support the abolitionists in Kansas.

men. The events of August 1855 would solidify Brown's reputation as a guerrilla war leader and the free-state hero of Bleeding Kansas, but at a terrible cost.

On August 25, 1855, a force of 250 heavily armed proslavery men marched toward Osawatomie. As they neared the town, they shot and killed Brown's son, Frederick. John Brown, with only about thirty men, rushed to defend the town. For about twenty minutes, Brown and his small group of men were able to fight off the entire proslavery force. Brown's forces were badly outnumbered, but Brown ran back and forth along his line of men, encouraging them to keep up the fight. Eventually Brown's forces were overrun. Brown was wounded, but he was able to escape.

Just outside of Osawatomie, John Brown watched the smoke coming from the burning town. With his son dead from a proslavery bullet, Brown proclaimed,

> I have only a short time to live—only one death to die, and I will die fighting for this cause. There will be no more peace in this land until slavery is done for. I will give them something else to do than to extend slave territory.[6]

John Brown was now going to take his fight to the South.

chapter four

HARPERS FERRY

HARPERS FERRY—After Osawatomie, John Brown participated in other small battles in Kansas. But the violence in Kansas was greatly reduced when the federal and state governments enforced a peace among the warring parties. In 1857 Brown returned to the East to gain support for his effort to take the "war" to the South. Some abolitionists saw Brown as a dangerous radical, but others considered him a great leader and supported his philosophy of ending slavery through violence. It was from these people that Brown was able to gain financial support. A secret committee of six wealthy and influential men was formed to support Brown financially. One of these supporters, Franklin B. Sanborn, would later write a popular book detailing the life of John Brown.

The committee thought that it was only financing more military raids in Kansas and Missouri. John Brown did go back to Kansas and Missouri on occasion to lead raids to free slaves, but all the while, he was planning an invasion in Virginia. Virginia was the most powerful state in the South. When the committee learned of Brown's plans, it was terrified. It threatened to withdraw its support if Brown continued his efforts to invade Virginia. Brown agreed not to invade, but in reality his agreement was only a postponement.

John Brown did not wait long. In spring 1859 he rented a farmhouse in Maryland, just across the Potomac River from Virginia, the heart of the South. From the farmhouse, Brown and his men prepared for their attack. The plan was to attack Harpers Ferry, Virginia, and take the federal weapons arsenal there. Brown expected hundreds of slaves to flock to the area as soon as they learned of the uprising, and he would then provide them with arms.

John Brown's plan was full of problems. It was essential that slaves come to the aid of Brown's force. But there was no real plan to alert the slaves to the attack. Brown was attacking a federal arsenal. He was attacking property of the United States government. He would not only have to contend with the state of Virginia, but also with the power of the United States Army.

On Sunday, October 16, 1859, Brown put his plan into action. Seventeen men, each armed with one rifle and two revolvers, crossed the Potomac River into Virginia. They cut telegraph lines so that the people of Harpers Ferry could not call for help. Brown and his men quickly and easily took the arsenal, capturing the surprised guards. Brown now had in his possession several million dollars' worth of weapons. All he needed was more men he could arm with the weapons and hostages for bargaining power.

Brown sent a number of his men deeper into Virginia to collect slaves and hostages. The first hostage was Colonel Lewis W. Washington, the great-grandnephew of George Washington. Washington and four of his slaves were forced back to Harpers Ferry with another hostage and six more of Washington's slaves. The confused slaves were then armed with spikes (long spearlike weapons).

The first day of Brown's war was over. Brown waited for slaves to flock to his aid; but none would come. The hostages were taken for the purpose of being exchanged for slaves. None would be exchanged.

Very early the next morning a freed slave working for the railroad approached Brown's men to see what was going on. Not realizing who he was, Brown's men shot him. He later died from his wounds. Ironically, a black man was the first person killed by Brown's men in their effort to free slaves. The shot alerted the rest of the town, which at this point did not know what had occurred at the arsenal. A train that Brown allowed to pass through the town alerted people outside of the town. By dawn, the governor of Virginia, Henry Wise, and the president of the United States, James Buchanan, knew of a slave revolt in Harpers Ferry. They did not yet know that it was John Brown who was leading the revolt.

Armed farmers and townspeople surrounded Brown and his men. Outnumbered and trapped, Brown sent a man out to convince the Virginians to allow Brown and his men to leave peacefully. The man was instead taken prisoner and brutally killed by an angry mob of Virginians.

A militia, or small group of citizen soldiers, from Maryland came to Harpers Ferry on the exaggerated report that 750 blacks and abolitionists had seized the town. Militias from Maryland and Virginia had arrived to support farmers and townspeople. The rest of that second day saw gunfire, resulting in a standoff and death on both sides. The popular mayor of Harpers Ferry, Fontaine Beckham, was shot and killed during the gunfire. John Brown retreated into a small firehouse with his surviving men and the hostages.

President Buchanan ordered Colonel Robert E. Lee to take command of the federal troops already on the way to Harpers Ferry. Lee was a brilliant commander who had fought in the Mexican-American War and would later become the commander of the Confederate (Southern) forces during the Civil War. Among the federal troops at his disposal was a company of Marines who were specifically trained for swift attacks.

By the end of that Monday, Brown saw how desperate his situation was. He and his men were trapped in the firehouse. Two of his sons were severely wounded and would die that night. Other men were dead or dying all around him. They had no food and were exhausted from the day's battle. Brown still had hope, however. The hostages were so far preventing the militia outside from storming the building. Perhaps he could still use them to negotiate a peace settlement. Brown did know that he was no longer dealing with a disorganized militia. Lee had arrived and taken command of all of the forces outside the firehouse.

That night, newspapers throughout the country reported a slave rebellion at Harpers Ferry. It was not yet reported, however, that the leader was John Brown. Many cities in the South, with the memory of Nat Turner's rebellion still lingering, stationed guards on the streets and confined slaves to their quarters. Southern papers greatly overestimated the number of men involved in the rebellion, reporting that hundreds were involved.

During the battle at Harpers Ferry, Brown was forced to retreat into a small firehouse with his surviving men and the hostages. The firehouse is shown here years later, as a tourist attraction.

When dawn came on Tuesday morning, Robert E. Lee was preparing to storm the firehouse, which his troops had surrounded the night before. The small brick building was only about thirty-five feet long and thirty feet deep. It had three large double doors in front, which Brown had blocked from inside. Lee ordered young officer Jeb Stuart to ask Brown to surrender but not to negotiate with him. Should Brown attempt to negotiate or refuse to surrender, the force of twenty-four Marines was to attack. To ensure that no hostages would be killed, Lee ordered the men not to fire their weapons but to attack with bayonets.

The Marines approached the firehouse. Jeb Stuart went to one of the doors and demanded John Brown's surrender. Brown attempted to negotiate a safe passage for his men. Following Lee's orders, Stuart gave the signal and the Marines burst into the firehouse. Brown's men began to shoot. The battle raged in the darkness of the firehouse for only a few seconds. Two Marines were hit, and two of Brown's men were bayoneted to death. Brown himself was beaten unconscious by Lieutenant Israel Green. Although beaten with a sword, Brown's wounds were not life threatening. All of the hostages were rescued.

Less than two days after it started, John Brown's slave revolt was over. Ten of his men were dead, including two of his sons. Five others were prisoners, and the rest had escaped for the time being. Brown's revolt was a military failure. But if Brown's goal was to end slavery, his military failure was the best thing that could have happened. The nation now knew who John Brown was and why he was at

Harpers Ferry. Brown would surely be put on trial, and this is when he would bring his message to the nation. Brown would not be the abolitionists' great general, but he could still be their greatest martyr, sacrificing his life for the cause. He could not free the slaves through a revolt, but perhaps if others saw his sacrifice they would be influenced to follow his cause.

John Brown knew that he now had the opportunity to make something out of nothing. His actions and statements over the next few weeks would show that he was well aware of his role in history, and he was now going to make the most of it. He first demonstrated his awareness only a few short hours after his capture.

Governor Wise and others questioned Brown a few hours after his capture. Brown lay on the floor in a building surrounded by politicians from both the North and the South. All were curious about his intentions. Brown was covered in blood and was still in pain from his wounds. When asked why he came to Harpers Ferry, an angry Brown answered, "We came to free the slaves." When asked why he felt justified in doing this, he shot back, "You are guilty of a great wrong against God and humanity and it would be perfectly right for any one to interfere with you so far as to free those you willfully and wickedly hold in bondage."[1]

As the questioning became more heated, Governor Wise interrupted and warned Brown that the statements he was making were incriminating. Wise said,

> You are suffering from wounds, perhaps fatal; and should you escape death from these causes, you must submit to a

trial which may involve death. Your confessions justify the presumption that you will be found guilty. . . . It better you should turn your attention to your eternal future than be dealing in denunciations which can only injure you.[2]

In a preview of the tactics that he would use in the trial to come, Brown turned the tables on the governor. In a calm voice, Brown warned Wise,

Governor, I have from all appearances not more than fifteen or twenty years the start of you in the journey to that eternity of which you kindly warn me. . . . The difference between your tenure and mine is trifling, and I therefore tell you to

After Brown refused to surrender, Robert E. Lee ordered the Marines to storm into the firehouse. The battle lasted only a few seconds. Two of Brown's men were killed and Brown was beaten unconscious.

be prepared. I am prepared. You all have a heavy responsibility, and it behooves you to prepare more than it does me.[3]

John Brown was prepared for his fate. He was warning the South to prepare to answer for the sin of slavery.

Even though Brown and his men were in custody, people of the South were fearful. Greatly exaggerated reports on the scope of the raid filled Southern newspapers. Militias were placed on alert and combed the land for suspected raiders from the North. None was found. The raid was, in fact, limited to Brown and his men. No troops from the North were preparing to invade the South. But this reality did nothing to ease the tension and fear in the South. In the trial to follow, the tension would only worsen.

In the North, the raid was widely condemned by the newspapers. But whereas the South condemned the raid as a crime, the North condemned it as an unacceptable means to a noble goal. John Brown intended to show the North that not only was it an acceptable means to a noble goal, but also was the *only* way to end slavery. The South was about to give Brown his platform to deliver that message.

chapter five

THE TRIAL BEGINS

CHARLESTON, VA—On October 25, at 10:30 A.M., John Brown and four of his men were brought before the court in Charleston, Virginia, for a preliminary hearing.

The Preliminary Hearing

A preliminary hearing is the first formal step in the trial process. The defendants, or the people charged, are informed of the charges against them. Bond, or bail, is a sum of money that is set by a judge and paid by the accused to assure that he or she will come to trial if released from prison before the trial. If the accused does not show up for trial, then the money is forfeited to the court and an order to find and arrest the accused is given. In most cases bond or bail is set at the preliminary hearing. If the accused cannot post bail, he or she must stay in jail until the trial begins. Because of the seriousness of the charges against Brown and his men, no bond was set. At the preliminary hearing the prosecution, in this case the state of Virginia, had to establish probable cause. That is, it had to show at least some evidence to support the charges. This is usually done with the testimony of only a few witnesses.

John Brown learned that he was charged with treason and murder. The court than asked Brown if he had an attorney. Brown replied,

> I did not ask for any quarter at the time I was taken. I did not ask to have my life spared. The Governor of the State of Virginia tendered me his assurance that I should have a fair trial; and under no circumstances whatever, will I be able to have a fair trial. If you seek my blood, you can have it at any moment, without this mockery of a trial. I have no counsel. I have not been able to advise with any one. There are mitigating circumstances that I would urge in our favor, if a fair trial is to be allowed us. But if we are to be forced with mere form—a trial for execution—you might spare yourselves that trouble. I am ready for my fate.[1]

John Brown realized that although Governor Wise assured him that he would be treated fairly, this would be impossible in Virginia or anywhere else in the South. He was telling the court that he knew that any trial under those circumstances was merely a formality before he was to be executed. He had no intention to deny the facts surrounding what happened at Harpers Ferry. What he wanted was an opportunity to tell the court and the rest of the country why he went to Harpers Ferry and what he intended to accomplish. In time, he would get his opportunity.

The court then appointed two local attorneys, Charles J. Faulkner and Lawson Botts, to represent John Brown and each of his men. Both lawyers reluctantly agreed to accept the court's appointment. They agreed because the court would have most likely ordered them to do so even if they declined. They were reluctant because of the enormous pressure that they would receive from their fellow Southerners for defending these men.

The court did not want future jurors to hear any evidence before the trial started. Therefore, it ordered the press not to report any details of the testimony that came out at the preliminary hearing.

With that instruction, the prosecution began to present its evidence. Its first witness was Lewis Washington, who detailed being taken and held hostage. Other hostages testified about their ordeal and the bloodshed they had witnessed. After the testimony, the court found that probable cause existed and sent the case to the Circuit Court of Jefferson County for possible indictment, or formal charges against the defendant.

The Indictment

An indictment is a formal charge of a crime. It can only be handed down by a grand jury. A grand jury is a group of citizens that hears evidence presented by the prosecution in a closed hearing. Unlike a petit jury in a trial, the grand jurors can ask questions directly of the witnesses. The defense presents no witnesses and is not permitted to even attend the proceeding. Like the judge in a preliminary hearing, the grand jury must decide whether there is probable cause to proceed to trial and what the exact charges against the defendants should be.

At 2:00 P.M. on the same day as the preliminary hearing, Judge Richard Parker summoned the grand jury to hear evidence. The grand jury, as did all Virginia juries, consisted of only white Southern men. The grand jury heard the prosecution's witnesses until 5:00 P.M., when it was released by the court and ordered to continue its examination at 10:00 A.M. the next day. Judge Parker ordered that John Brown have no further access to reporters, who were eager to hear his story. The judge feared that Brown would still be able to influence others into uprising, which, of course, was Brown's intention.

Crowds of people from around the country began to gather in Charleston. Like the high-profile trials of today, small groups of reporters gathered. Couriers and telegraphs were the only ways to send the reporters' stories back to their local papers. Fearing either an attempted rescue from Northern supporters or an attempted lynching from angry Southerners, security was extremely high. Manned cannons were even placed in front of the courthouse.

The next morning the grand jury continued its examination of witnesses. At noon the jury returned an indictment against Brown and his men. The indictment read,

> John Brown, Aaron C. Stephens,. . . together with diverse other evil-minded and traitorous persons to the Jurors unknown, not having the fear of God before their eyes, but moved and seduced by the false and malignant counsel of the other evil and traitorous persons and the instigators of the devil, did . . . with other confederates to the Jurors

unknown, feloniously and traitorously make rebellion and
levy war against the said Commonwealth of Virginia.[2]

Brown had been indicted for treason, first-degree murder, and insurrection. Each charge was punishable by death.

The grand jury's indictment, and more specifically the wording of the indictment, echoed feelings of many in the South. The grand jury and many Southerners felt that Brown and his men were "evil and traitorous." Brown's motive for the rebellion—to free slaves—was seen not only as an illegal act but also as one that amounted to war against Virginia. The motive was also seen as going against the will of God and as being evil. It was clear in the minds of the grand jurors and most Southerners that John Brown and his men had not acted alone. They specifically mentioned "other evil and traitorous persons" besides Brown and his men. In the minds of Southerners, this was a Northern conspiracy to end the Southern way of life.

When the news of John Brown's capture and indictment reached his financial backers in the North, they panicked. Most feared that documents taken from Brown would incriminate them, and they fled to Canada. In fact, some letters from Franklin B. Sanborn and other abolitionist supporters of Brown were confiscated from Brown's Maryland farmhouse. It is not clear exactly how much these "conspirators" knew about the raid but it was enough to send most of them into hiding—at least for a short time. Even though Frederick Douglass was opposed to the raid, he, too, fled to England until the situation cooled.

The Arraignment

That afternoon John Brown and his men were brought back to the courtroom for the arraignment. An arraignment takes place after the indictment. The indictment is read to the defendants, and they plead either guilty or not guilty to the charges. By this time Charles Faulkner, who had been reluctant to represent Brown at the preliminary hearing, had declined to represent him. Lawson Botts, who was now working alone, asked the court to appoint his assistant, Thomas C. Green to aid in Brown's defense. Judge Parker agreed.

The stage was set. All parties were present. Judge Parker would preside over the case. The judge came from a family with a long line of judges. He was well respected and equally intimidating.

Prosecuting for the state of Virginia was Charles Harding. Harding was the prosecutor in the town of Harpers Ferry, where Brown's raid had taken place. As the local prosecutor, Harding was automatically assigned to the case. Harding's ability as an attorney, however, was in question. His suit was dirty, his hair was uncombed, and his face was covered with unshaven stubble.[3] Harding was in drastic contrast to his cocounsel, Andrew Hunter. Governor Wise was unimpressed with Harding's abilities and appointed Hunter as special counsel for the state of Virginia to assist in the prosecution of Brown. Hunter was an attractive, well-respected, Southern gentleman who would certainly appeal to any Southern jury.

John Brown was well represented. Lawson Botts was

Colonel Robert E. Lee was the commander of the federal troops at Harpers Ferry. He later commanded the Confederate forces during the Civil War.

thirty-six years old and had a reputation as a fine attorney. His assistant, Thomas C. Green, was the mayor of Charleston.

Brown would be tried in Charleston, Virginia, which is today Charleston, West Virginia. The courtroom was primitive by today's standards. The floor was covered with peanut shells, and the white walls were smudged with fingerprints. The spectators sat on benches filled beyond capacity by five to six hundred people.

The prisoners were forced to stand as the indictment, or list of formal charges, was read. Standing was not easy, though, as some of the prisoners were still suffering from the wounds inflicted at Harpers Ferry. Two bailiffs assisted Aaron Stevens, who was lying on a cot for most of the hearing. As the indictment was read, each prisoner, including John Brown, pleaded not guilty.

Each prisoner also requested a separate trial. This would enable each prisoner to choose his own defense and strategy for trial. If tried together, their defenses would conflict, and they would end up arguing against each other rather than against the prosecution. The court granted the request for separate trials, and the prosecution elected to try John Brown first.

Brown rose before the indictment was read and said: "I do not intend to detain the Court, but barely wish to say I have been promised a fair trial, that I am not now in circumstances that do not enable me to attend a trial, owing to the state of my health."[4] Botts also requested a short delay of the trial so that Brown could retain attorneys of his choice to defend him. Hunter objected to a delay in trial, stating that it would "give strength to our enemies abroad."[5] The state of Virginia still had a real fear that an attempt to free Brown might be underway.

The court called the doctor who had treated Brown to ask about the seriousness of Brown's injuries. The doctor stated that Brown's injuries were not serious and would not affect his ability to help his attorneys in defending himself. The court then denied the request to delay the trial. The trial of John Brown began immediately.

Day One

The jury selection process began at 2:00 P.M. on October 26. A panel of potential jurors was brought into the courtroom. The judge and attorney questioned each potential juror individually on his ability to hear the case and decide John Brown's fate fairly and impartially. If any juror indicated an inability to be fair or a predisposition toward Brown's guilt, that person would be dismissed. The process of questioning potential jurors is called *voir dire*, a Latin phrase meaning "to tell the truth." It is the process during which the court and the attorneys choose a jury. The ultimate goal is to choose a jury that can be fair and impartial.

John Brown was ordered into court, but he refused to rise, claiming he was not able to walk. He was then carried into court on a cot and placed on the floor. Any jurors who were present at Harpers Ferry during the raid were excused. Each of those who remained were then questioned on what they had heard about the case and if they could be fair and impartial. Once twenty-four jurors were qualified, Botts was allowed to eliminate eight jurors who he felt would be prejudiced against his client. The remaining sixteen were chosen from a ballot. The jury consisted of twelve white Southern men. Some of the jurors were slave owners.

The court instructed the jurors not to discuss the case with anyone and not to allow anyone to discuss the case with them. The court then adjourned until the next morning.

Day Two

Lawson Botts read to the court a telegram that he had received that morning from a man in Akron, Ohio, who was familiar with the Brown family;

> Insanity is hereditary in that family. His [John Brown's] mother's sister died with it, and a daughter of that sister has been two years in a Lunatic Asylum. A son and a daughter of his mother's brother have has also been confined in the lunatic asylum, and another son of that brother is now insane and under close restraint. These facts can be conclusively proven by witnesses residing here, who will doubtless attend the trial if desired.[6]

Botts then told the court that John Brown had informed him that he did not, however, wish to plead insanity. Brown himself then stood and told the court, "I am perfectly unconscious of insanity, and I reject, so far as I am capable, any attempt to interfere in my behalf on that score."[7]

Botts did not push the insanity defense for two reasons. First, Brown did not want him to. If Brown plead not guilty by reason of insanity, he would, in effect, be implying that his actions at Harpers Ferry were insane. The last thing that

Brown wanted anyone to infer was that the idea of freeing the slaves by violent means was an insane act.

Second, even by today's standards, John Brown's conduct would probably not amount to legal insanity. Being "mentally ill" and "not guilty by reason of insanity" are entirely different things. The latter is a legal definition. Someone can be mentally ill and still be legally responsible for his or her conduct. Today, in most states, to prove a person not guilty by reason of insanity, the defense has to prove one of two things: that the person was in such a mental state at the time of the crime that he or she could not appreciate the wrongfulness (illegality) of the act or that the person lacked the ability of preventing himself or herself from committing the act. Brown knew what he was doing was illegal and he chose to do it despite this fact. Furthermore, Brown's conduct was carefully planned and not merely an irresistible impulse that he could not control.

A telegram indicated that Brown's new attorneys were on their way to Charleston. Botts then requested that the court delay starting the trial so that Brown could have his own attorneys represent him. Andrew Hunter stood and again objected to any continuance. Hunter implied that the real reason for the request was to allow time for Northerners to come rescue Brown. Thomas Green replied that they needed a day to see if Brown's attorneys were, in fact, on their way. The court refused the request and read the oath to the jurors, who all swore to try the defendant fairly and impartially.

The seven-page indictment, or formal charges, of treason,

insurrection, and murder, was then read to the jury as Brown lay on the cot.

The State of Virginia Addresses the Court

Prosecutor Charles Harding first addressed the jury. He laid out the facts, as the jury would hear them from the witnesses. He told them about the evidence that the state would present. He defined the offenses and assured the jury that the prosecution would indeed prove each offense beyond a reasonable doubt.

The Opening Statement for Brown

Defense attorney Thomas Green then addressed the jury. He reminded the jurors that the defendant was innocent until proven guilty. If they had doubt about guilt, he told them that they must give the benefit of that doubt to the defendant. Green also instructed the jurors that a conviction for treason could not be made based on a confession given outside the courtroom; only a confession in the courtroom could be used for a conviction. This last point was important because of the incriminating statements made by Brown when he was questioned shortly after his capture.

Regarding the charge of insurrection, Green hinted that the court did not have jurisdiction and thus could not convict Brown of this charge. Jurisdiction means that a court can only hear cases that a law or constitution allows them to hear. Laws usually limit a court's jurisdiction geographically. For example, a state court can only hear a criminal case for crimes committed within its borders. Laws can also limit a court's jurisdiction by subject matter. For example, a state court cannot hear a case based on a federal law. Federal laws are limited to federal courts.

Regarding the charge of murder, Green told the jury that they must find that it was deliberate and premeditated, otherwise, the proper conviction was second-degree murder, which was not punishable by death.

Lawson Botts then stood and gave his opening on behalf of John Brown. He asked the jury to put aside their prejudices against the North and to calmly judge the defendant. He reminded the jurors that the burden of proof was on the state and not on the defendant. Addressing the issue of jurisdiction, he argued that the state of Virginia had no right to try Brown. Since the entire event took place in a federal arsenal, this was a federal matter to be tried in a federal court, not a Virginia court. He told the jurors that the evidence would show that Brown treated his prisoners very well and with the utmost respect. He further stated that if Brown had intended to murder with malice, he would not have treated his hostages with such kindness. Botts also argued that treason usually required that the accused be a citizen of the state he is committing treason against, and Brown was not a citizen of Virginia.

The Prosecution's Opening Statement

Andrew Hunter then gave his opening statement for the state of Virginia. He explained his role as an assistant to the prosecution and a representative of Governor Wise. He went on to dispute the defense's position on the law. Although he

Virginia governor Henry Wise assured John Brown that he would get a fair trial, but Brown knew that was impossible in a Southern state.

recognized that this was the first time that Virginia had prosecuted anyone for treason, he also implied that if the jury did not convict Brown, it would not be the last time. Hunter explained that the requirement, in reference to convicting for treason solely on confessions in open court, applied only to federal treason, as it stated in the United States Constitution. John Brown was charged with treason under Virginia law, which was different and more comprehensive. Hunter claimed that the prosecution would show that Brown had attempted to overthrow the government of Virginia and replace it with his own. With regard to the jurisdiction question, Hunter appealed to the jury's contempt for the federal government, which many Southerners felt favored the North. He claimed that Virginia law applied to all property within the state, and Harpers Ferry was within its borders. As to murder, Hunter stated that the evidence would show that Brown not only personally engaged in murder but also directed others to commit the same.

The court then adjourned for the morning.

The Prosecution's Case

The court resumed the case that afternoon, and the prosecution called its first witness. Direct examination of witnesses is conducted by the side that calls a witness to the stand. Cross-examination of a witness is conducted by the opposing side. Dr. Starry took the witness stand. On direct examination, Starry testified about the first shots heard at Harpers Ferry. Starry lived at Harpers Ferry and was awakened by gunfire late Sunday night. As he investigated, he saw an exchange of gunfire between some of John Brown's men and the men at the armory gate near the railroad bridge. The bridge lies across the river between Maryland and Virginia. He testified that he saw a train at the end of the bridge across from the armory and a black man who had been shot. Confused and alarmed, the doctor said he saw strange men patrolling the area the rest of the night. Early Monday morning, he warned as many people as he could in Harpers Ferry. Later, he rode to Charleston to alert the authorities. He then rode back to Harpers Ferry to assist in the attack to take back the armory. Throughout the entire time, he did not personally see John Brown.

Dr. Starry lived on the Maryland side of the bridge across from the armory. On cross-examination, Thomas Green was able to bring out through Starry's testimony that Starry would have had to pass Brown's men on the other side of the bridge in order to alert the authorities in Charleston. Starry testified that Brown's men did allow him to pass over the bridge without being fired on.

The prosecution's next witness, Andrew Phelps, was the conductor of the train that Starry mentioned during his testimony. Phelps testified that as his train approached Harpers Ferry, he noticed that there was no watchman on the armory bridge. He thought this was strange but started to cross the bridge anyway. Just then, the watchman appeared. He ran up to the train and told Phelps that he was attacked by a number of armed men who now had control of the armory.

Phelps testified that he decided to cross the bridge

slowly. He and a few others from the train walked in front, and the engineer followed in the train. As they crossed, Phelps heard someone from the other side yell to them to stop and identify themselves. He then immediately saw four rifles through the darkness pointing at him. He yelled to the engineer to back up the train and ran back to the other side. As he did this he heard gunfire, then he saw a black man named Hayword run toward him, saying that he had been shot. The man had been shot in the back, and the bullet had passed through the front of his chest. They retreated to the other side of the bridge. Phelps carried Hayword to the railroad house and summoned Dr. Starry. Hayword died shortly thereafter.

Phelps further testified that, after an exchange of gunfire between Phelps's party and Brown's men, a man from the other side of the bridge had yelled out that the train could now pass over the bridge. Phelps wisely yelled back, "I would rather not, after these proceedings," then he asked the unknown man, "What do you want?" The man had responded, "We want liberty, and we intend to have it." When Phelps asked, "What do you mean?" he replied, "You will find out in a day or two."[8] To protect the passengers, Phelps decided to wait until daylight to pass over the bridge.

The rest of the night he watched what he estimated to be about thirty men near the firehouse at the other side of the river busily preparing for something. The next morning he approached Brown's men and learned that they were there to free the slaves. Brown apologized for the events the night before and told him that he did not intend for there to be any bloodshed. According to Phelps, Brown then assured safe passage for the train and even accompanied him and his train across the bridge. The train passed through Harpers Ferry unharmed.

Andrew Phelps returned to Harpers Ferry the next day and was present when Governor Wise questioned John Brown shortly after he was captured. Phelps testified about what he heard. Phelps said Brown spoke of taking the armory in order to arm the two thousand men he expected to rally to his cause. Brown told the governor that he was the commander in chief of a provisional government and that they had adopted a constitution. A provisional government is a temporary government meant to deal with the immediate situation until an elected government can be formed. A copy of the provisional government's constitution was captured during the raid of the firehouse.

Thomas Green realized that this testimony was very damaging to Brown because it related to treason and insurrection. Green stood up and interrupted the testimony. He told the court that he had just received a message that Brown's attorneys were on their way and would be in Charleston that night. He asked the court to adjourn, or stop, for the day so that the attorneys Brown wanted could cross-examine this important witness. Once again Andrew Hunter objected, and once again the court refused to delay.

As the trial continued, Green cross-examined Phelps. Phelps appeared to be very honest and not to hold a grudge against Brown. He told the jury that Brown said he was sorry for the gunfire on the bridge and that he did not order the attack. Brown expressed to Phelps that he did not wish bloodshed and that it would not happen again provided he was not attacked. Green was also able to make the point, through Phelps, that John Brown was not personally involved in the shooting. Phelps said he would have noticed Brown due to his long beard.

The prosecution's next witness was Lewis W. Washington. Because Washington was a member of a prominent Virginia family, great care was taken by both the prosecution and the defense to treat him with the utmost respect. Washington testified that he was asleep at his house about 1:00 A.M. Monday when he was awakened by a noise. He thought he heard someone call his name. When he went downstairs to investigate, he found himself surrounded by six of Brown's men. Washington did not meet Brown until he was he was taken, along with two of his slaves, to Harpers Ferry. There, he was held as a hostage. Washington went on to detail all the events leading up to the Marines storming the firehouse.

On cross-examination by Green, Washington said he could not tell whether the Marines fired their weapons when they stormed the building. He testified that the noise was too great and it was extremely dark and smoky inside. Knowing that an attack on the firehouse was about to come, Washington said John Brown put them in a safer place in the back.

On redirect examination by Hunter, Washington discussed the questioning by Governor Wise. Washington repeated many of the same things that Phelps had heard. He specifically heard John Brown tell Governor Wise that he chose Harpers Ferry as the place he planned to establish his provisional government. According to Washington, Brown made it perfectly clear that his intentions were to free the slaves.

Lawson Botts questioned the witness to show that John Brown wished no harm to his hostages. Washington said it was Brown who told the hostages to go to the rear of the firehouse before the attack. Brown also ordered his men not to fire on any unarmed men.

Charles Harding then established that the slaves were, in fact, hostages, too. Washington testified that although John Brown armed the captured slaves with spears, they did not appear to be voluntarily taking up arms. He said that one even escaped and returned home.

As Washington testified, a young attorney from Boston was approaching Charleston. George H. Hoyt, only twenty-one years old, was hired by Brown's Northern supporters to defend him. Hoyt was also hired to find out just how much evidence existed to incriminate the Northern supporters. As the evening approached, the court adjourned for the day. Washington would continue his testimony the next day.

Day Three

The next morning George Hoyt appeared in court with Lawson Botts and Thomas Green. Andrew Hunter demanded that Hoyt show some proof that he was qualified to practice law. Hoyt failed to bring any with him. After a brief discussion, Green was able to assure Judge Parker that

Hoyt was, in fact, a practicing lawyer in Boston. The judge then permitted Hoyt to assist in John Brown's defense.

Lawson Botts continued to cross-examine Washington. He questioned him on the negotiations during the siege. This questioning was intended to show that Brown wanted a peaceful resolution. Washington said that negotiations for the release of the hostages began on Monday, after Brown had retreated to the firehouse. According to Washington, Brown wanted merely to get out of Harpers Ferry by this time. He said that Brown offered to leave the firehouse and free the hostages in return for safe passage over the bridge.

Brown's wife, Mary, arrives at the Charleston courthouse in a horse-drawn carriage, for her husband's trial.

Brown would cross the bridge with the hostages, and once he got to the other side, he would free them. This plan was apparently rejected by the Virginians.

Washington went on to recount the events in the firehouse. He remembered Brown's son being shot through the chest during the battle shortly before the Marines attacked. Although he was badly wounded, Brown's son kept firing his gun until pain forced him to stop. Once the Marines did attack, Brown and his men kept fighting. They ignored the calls for surrender. Washington said that Brown had a rifle in his hands when he was finally struck down and captured by Lieutenant Israel Green.

Once Washington was finished with his testimony, Hunter presented the written constitution and other documents of Brown's provisional government. Hunter called Sheriff Campbell, who was holding Brown prisoner, to verify that the handwriting on the documents was, in fact, Brown's. Campbell had seen Brown's handwriting from letters Brown had written in jail. Brown told the court and Hunter that he would be willing to identify the documents as his. But Hunter, not wanting Brown to appear honest in front of the jury, had Campbell identify the documents instead. After Campbell identified each document, it was then handed to Brown and his attorneys. As this was done, to be sure the jury would hear, Brown would loudly proclaim each document to be his.

The prosecution's next witness was Armstead Ball. Ball was a machinist at the armory and one of Brown's first hostages. When captured at the armory, Brown told Ball that he was there to free the slaves and did not want war on the people, only against the system of slavery. Brown allowed Ball to return home under guard to tell his family that he would be all right. He was escorted back to the armory after this visit but was allowed a second visit later that day. The remainder of his testimony on direct examination mirrored Washington's.

Thomas Green cross-examined Armstead Ball to show that John Brown did not want any harm to come to the hostages. This backfired, though. Ball instead said that when the Marines attacked, Brown had used the hostages as a shield. Although some of Brown's men quietly urged the hostages to take cover in the back, Brown did not. This directly contradicted Washington's testimony.

John Allstadt was next to take the stand. He stated that at about 3:00 A.M. on Monday he was awakened from his sleep by several of Brown's men and forced downstairs. He was told that they were there to free the slaves. He and seven of his slaves were put in a wagon and brought to Harpers Ferry. Once at Harpers Ferry, his slaves were armed with spears. By this time Washington was already captured. Brown told Washington and Allstadt that he intended to release them in return for two slaves from the outside. As it turns out, the Virginians refused to exchange slaves for any of the hostages.

Allstadt's testimony was similar to Washington's. When asked about the captured slaves, he said that they had dropped their spears and some had slept through most of the ordeal. This testimony brought laughter from the audience and the jury. When the Marines attacked, Allstadt claimed that Brown was in the front, firing his gun at the Marines. Allstadt believed that Brown had killed one Marine.

On cross-examination, Thomas Green forced Allstadt to admit that he could not state for sure that it was John Brown's shot that killed the Marine. He stated that many people were firing and that it was very confusing. He also stated that the Marines did fire their weapons, but only after being fired on by Brown and his men.

The next few witnesses called by the prosecution were members of various militias. They had forced Brown and his men to retreat to the firehouse. One of those people was Henry Hunter, the son of special prosecutor Andrew Hunter. Each of the militia members testified that they exchanged gunfire with Brown and his men for the better part of Monday. A number of men in the militia were killed or wounded in the battle. They were also able to kill and capture a number of Brown's men. That evening Colonel Robert E. Lee arrived and took command of the situation.

The prosecution rested. It appeared that Hunter had, in fact, proven his case. If John Brown did not personally fire a shot that killed anyone, there was evidence that the men under his command did. Under the law, Brown was responsible. Concerning treason and insurrection, the witnesses testified that Brown was at Harpers Ferry to free the slaves. The prosecution was able to obtain testimony about Brown's statements to Governor Wise. Most damaging of all, the prosecution was able to get into evidence a copy of the constitution for Brown's provisional government.

It was now Lawson Botts's turn to present evidence for Brown's defense. The only real victory Brown's attorneys could hope for was to keep John Brown from being killed. The plan was simply to show that Brown treated his hostages well and wanted as little bloodshed as possible. If they could do this, it was possible that the jury would only convict on second-degree murder. This would save Brown from the hangman's noose. But although Brown wanted to show that he treated his hostages well, he did not want his life to be saved.

chapter six

THE CASE FOR THE DEFENSE

COURTHOUSE—John Brown's attorneys wanted to present as much evidence as possible showing that Brown treated his hostages well under the circumstances. In the end, this strategy would backfire. The circumstances under which Brown placed the hostages were so terrible that the jury would give little weight to any kindness Brown showed at Harpers Ferry.

The first witness for the defense was Joseph A. Brewer, who had been a hostage during the raid. He, too, testified about the odd combination of kindness and ruthlessness that Brown demonstrated throughout the ordeal. He told the jury that Brown was very polite and seemed to want as little bloodshed as possible. But he also confirmed Allstadt's testimony that Brown intended the hostages to be used as shields.

Brewer said that on a number of occasions Brown sent men out under a white flag in an attempt to negotiate with the militias. Each time, Brown's men were fired on. In the last such attempt, Brown sent one of his men, Aaron Stevens, and a hostage named A. M. Kitzmiller. The militia, consisting of angry citizens from the area, fired on them, striking Stevens. Stevens was lying outside the firehouse badly wounded and in obvious pain. Brown refused to send any of his men out to assist him in fear that they would be shot, too.

Brewer, who could hear the groans coming from Stevens, asked Brown if he could go out and carry Stevens to a safe place were he could be treated. With a promise from Brewer that he would return to his captors, Brown agreed. The brave Brewer, not knowing if his fellow citizens would fire on him, left the firehouse and carried Stevens to a nearby building. Incredibly, Brewer kept his word and returned to the firehouse and remained a hostage until rescued by the Marines.

Seeing that the witnesses were having little effect gaining the jury's sympathy for Brown, Botts and Green decided to go on the offensive. They intended to present evidence that the Virginians were guilty of their own wrongdoing at Harpers Ferry.

A. M. Kitzmiller was called to the stand. Kitzmiller testified that Brown had asked him to use his influences with the local citizens, who had Brown trapped in the firehouse. He confirmed Brewer's testimony that he was sent out with Stevens to try to negotiate with a group of militia stationed on the bridge overlooking the firehouse. Stevens carried his rifle with him. As the two approached, one of the militiamen remarked to Stevens that he should have left his gun behind. Kitzmiller then waved his handkerchief and told Stevens to stay behind as he approached the men. As he did this, he heard a shot, turned, and saw that Stevens was struck. Stevens returned the fire. Kitzmiller did not see who had shot Stevens. Kitzmiller wisely did not return to the firehouse.

Kitzmiller was questioned about what happened to William Thompson, another of Brown's men. Kitzmiller said that the last time he saw Thompson, Thompson had been taken prisoner by the same men he had approached on the bridge. He stated that Thompson was captured at about the same time that Mayor Beckham was killed.

Thomas Green asked the court if he could introduce testimony relating to the death of Thompson. Andrew Hunter objected, stating that it was not relevant to the conduct of John Brown. Hunter felt that because Brown was on trial and not the militiamen, the conduct of Brown alone was at issue. Although Hunter did not at all approve of the killing of Thompson, he argued that it had nothing to do with the crimes charged against Brown. Green told the court that he wanted to introduce this evidence to show that, despite the brutal murder of Thompson, Brown did not treat the hostages cruelly. Hunter responded that there was no point to this unless the defense could show that Brown knew that Thompson was killed after he was captured. Botts reminded the court that the defense had already proven that there was communication between the parties for hours after Thompson's death. The court overruled Hunter's objection and allowed Green to proceed with the evidence.

The defense called Andrew Hunter's own son, Henry,

back to the witness stand, this time to testify for the defense. The prosecutor could only listen while his son recited the terrible details involving the murder of Thompson by the angry citizens of Harpers Ferry. The testimony would reveal that Henry Hunter personally had a hand in the murder.

The militia captured Thompson, like Stevens, when he was sent out by John Brown to negotiate. Not long after his capture, the popular mayor Fontaine Beckham was killed by Brown's men during an exchange of gunfire. Henry Hunter testified:

> After Mr. Beckham, who was my grand-uncle, was shot, I was much exasperated and started with Mr. Chambers [another militiaman] to the room where the second Thompson was confined, with the purpose of shooting him. We found several persons in the room, and had leveled our guns at him, when [one of the women] threw herself before him, and begged us to leave him to the laws. We then caught hold of him, and dragged him out by the throat, he saying: "Though you may take my life, Eighty million will rise up to avenge me, and carry out my purpose of giving liberty to the slaves." We carried him out to the bridge, and two of us, leveling our guns in this moment of wild exasperation, fired, and before he fell, a dozen or more balls were buried in him; we then threw his body off the tresses work, and returned to the bridge to bring out the prisoner, Stevens, and serve him the same way; we found him suffering from his wounds, and probably dying; we concluded to spare him, and start after others, and shot down by those villainous Abolitionists, and felt justified in shooting any that I could find; I felt it my duty, and I have no regrets.[1]

Dead silence fell over the courtroom as Hunter testified. Brown was heard crying as the details of Thompson's death

This picture of John Brown was taken in 1859, the year of his trial and his death. During his trial, Brown's attorneys wanted to prove that he had treated his hostages well.

were disclosed. It was now clear that there was brutality by both sides. But would this have any effect on the jury? Most of the jurors knew at least someone who was at Harpers Ferry during the raid. They were, of course, Southern men who, in all likelihood, agreed with Hunter's views on the "villainous abolitionists."

The defense called a number of other witnesses who confirmed that Brown was looking for a way out of Harpers Ferry without bloodshed.

Brown, who was lying on a cot throughout the day's testimony, suddenly rose. He angrily said,

> May it please the Court: I discover that notwithstanding all the assurances I have received of a fair trial, nothing like a fair trial is to be given me, as it would seem. I gave the names, as soon as I could get them, of the persons I wished to have called as witnesses, and was assured that they would be subpoenaed. It appears they have not been subpoenaed as far as I can learn; and I now ask, if I am to have anything at all deserving the name and shadow of a fair trial, that this proceeding be deferred until tomorrow morning; for I have no counsel, as I before stated, in whom I feel that I can rely, but I am in hopes counsel may arrive who will attend to seeing that I get the witnesses who are necessary for my defense.[2]

After his speech, John Brown lay back down on the cot and appeared to go to sleep. He had made it clear that he felt that he neither had the witnesses he needed nor the attorneys he desired to defend himself. He wanted more time to enable Hoyt to prepare a defense and to secure the needed witnesses.

John Brown had given a list of witnesses to Lawson

Botts, and Botts subpoenaed those witnesses to court. A subpoena is a court order compelling a witness to give testimony in a case. Once the subpoena is served (delivered by some official), then that witness must comply or be arrested and forced to testify. The sheriff who was responsible for serving the subpoenas assured the court that they were served. In fact, some of those witnesses appeared and had already testified. Brown never specifically stated to the court which witnesses he wanted to appear.

With his statement, Brown managed to anger every person in the courtroom and to put himself in an even worse position than before. The prosecution did not want any further delays in the trial. The judge, whose job it was to see that Brown had a fair trial, was told in effect that he was not doing his job. Brown's own attorneys, Botts and Green, were told by their client that he had no confidence in their skills. Finally, Hoyt realized that in all likelihood he was now on his own. Exhausted from his journey, Hoyt was now put in a position of defending a client he had just met, in a trial that was halfway through, in a state with laws that were unfamiliar to him. To top all of that, he would have to do all of this as a Northerner in a Southern courtroom.

George Hoyt asked the court for a postponement until the next morning. He explained that yet another attorney, Judge D. R. Tilden from Ohio, would arrive that night to assist. He pleaded with the court,

> For myself, I have come from Boston, traveling night and day, to volunteer my services in defense of Brown. I could not undertake the responsibility of his defense, as I am now

situated. The gentlemen who have defended Brown acted in an honorable and dignified manner in all respects, so far as I know, but I cannot assume the responsibility of defending him myself. . . . I have not read the indictment through— have not . . . any idea of the line of defense proposed, and have no knowledge of the criminal code of Virginia.[3]

Lawson Botts and Thomas Green had risked their careers, reputations, and perhaps even their lives as Southern men representing this "villainous abolitionist." They met their ethical duty and represented Brown against the charges in the indictment. But John Brown did not want to defend himself against the indictment; he simply wanted to justify his actions against slavery.

Thomas Green rose and told the court that "Mr. Botts and myself will now withdraw from the case, as we can no longer act on behalf of the prisoner, he having got up now and declared here that he has no confidence in the counsel who have been assigned him."[4]

The court had before it the request from George Hoyt to postpone until the next day. Charles Harding had objected to any delay.

Botts rose one last time to assist his reluctant client. Botts suggested to the court that it should retire for the evening. This would allow him to assist Hoyt in preparing for the trial and educating him about the laws of Virginia. This would also give the sheriff time to get the other witnesses to court by the next day.

The court excused Thomas Green and Lawson Botts from the case and postponed the trial until the next morning.

Day Four

George Hoyt spent the night learning Virginia law from Lawson Botts. Judge Tilden had not shown up in Charleston, but two very respected attorneys had. The first was Hiram Griswald of Cleveland, and the second was Samuel Chilton of Washington, D.C. Chilton was originally from Virginia and had an excellent reputation as an attorney. He was hired by a wealthy Boston abolitionist for a fee of one thousand dollars—a great deal of money in those days.

On the day that the trial was to continue, the judge delayed the start for a few minutes so that he could meet Brown's new attorneys. When the trial resumed, Chilton stood and told the court that he came with the understanding that he was going to assist the attorneys who had previously been trying the case. Since those attorneys were no longer on the case, he requested a postponement so that he could review the charges. The judge, who was now dealing with Brown's sixth attorney, refused to postpone the case any longer.

George Hoyt had objected to some of the documents that the prosecution wished to introduce as evidence the day before. Andrew Hunter, clearly tired of the delays in the trial, withdrew some of those documents.

As Hoyt began to call witnesses who repeated the testimony of the previous witnesses, Hunter objected. Hunter complained that the defense was going over the same facts already testified to and suggested that it was stalling. Hunter still felt that John Brown was merely buying time so that a rescue attempt could be made.

Hoyt responded that he was trying to show an absence of malicious intention. That is, he wanted to show that Brown had no intention of causing pain or distress to his victims. He also told the court that he was questioning these witnesses on Brown's request. Judge Parker allowed Hoyt to continue.

Hoyt's next witness was hostage John P. Dangerfield. Dangerfield, too, testified that he was well treated by Brown. He also talked about the death of Brown's two sons. The first son was shot in the firehouse. The second was shot outside under a flag of truce. When Dangerfield saw him retreat to the firehouse, he was vomiting blood.

This jail in Charleston is the one where Brown was held prisoner from his capture in October 1859 to his death in December.

Hoyt put other witnesses on the stand who all had similar testimony. On one occasion Brown interrupted Hoyt and asked the witness whether he saw any firing by Brown that was not purely defensive. The witness responded, "It might be considered in that light, perhaps; the balls came into the engine house pretty thick."[5]

The prosecution did not even cross-examine the witnesses that Brown insisted Hoyt call to the stand. Whereas some of these witnesses testified that Brown treated them well, they also helped the prosecution in proving insurrection, treason, and murder. It seemed important to John Brown to show that he came to Harpers Ferry to free slaves. He did not wish bloodshed, but he was prepared to use violence if necessary. He also wanted to show the sacrifice he made for his cause. His two sons were dead, and he had no doubt about his own similar fate.

Brown never testified in his own defense. This is noteworthy but not particularly unusual. In any court case, the prosecution has the burden of proving its case beyond reasonable doubt. The defendant—in this case, John Brown—does not have to do or prove anything. In addition, Brown was convinced that his actions were justified. As a result, he most likely did not feel a need to defend himself or his actions.

Closing Arguments

The defense had run out of witnesses. There was to be no more testimony. It was time for closing arguments. A closing argument is a statement by the attorneys that explains how the evidence in the trial proved or disproved a particular fact. Although it is not new evidence, it is meant to persuade the jury to see the evidence from the point of view of the side making the argument. It is the last chance the attorneys have to talk to the jury. Since the prosecution has the burden of proof, it is allowed to go first; then, after the defense gives its closing argument, the prosecution is allowed to give a second closing argument.

John Brown was in a bad position. He had fired the only attorneys who had heard all the evidence. George Hoyt had heard some evidence, but he was physically exhausted. In the last five days, he had had a total of only ten hours of sleep and he had been up the entire night before learning about Virginia law. Samuel Chilton and Hiram Griswald had only heard that day's testimony and certainly could not argue about evidence they had not heard.

Brown's only chance for anything that resembled a closing argument was another postponement. But it was Saturday, and Judge Parker wanted to end the trial that night. The jurors were sequestered (not allowed to speak to anyone and kept under guard until a verdict was reached), and under Virginia law, they could not try the case on a Sunday. If another continuance were granted, the jurors would have to spend the weekend away from their families.

Hiram Griswald stood and asked the court for yet another postponement so "counsel could obtain sufficient knowledge of the evidence previously taken by reading notes of it."[6] He suggested that the prosecution give its closing statement that night. He would wait to give his closing until Monday. This was a highly unusual request, because the prosecution in a case always has the first and last word with the jury.

Andrew Hunter objected, stating that it was Brown's own fault that he had unprepared attorneys. After all, he had dismissed his previous attorneys. He added that it was Brown who, by his delaying tactics, had kept the jury away from their families and that, under the circumstances, "there could not be a female in this county who, whether with the good cause or not, was not trembling with anxiety and apprehension."[7]

Hunter was accurate in his statement that Brown had been delaying the trial. It was Brown who insisted that witnesses who gave no additional information, and even hurt his case, be called. It was Brown who fired his attorneys near the end of the trial. From time to time, Brown would not leave his jail cell to come to court, claiming his injuries were too serious. Brown's doctor said he was faking and there was no medical reason why Brown could not enter the courtroom by his own power.

It is unclear why John Brown wanted to delay the trial. Perhaps he simply wanted to give attorneys or witnesses time to get to Charleston. It could also have been that Brown was still hoping for a slave uprising that never came.

The judge reluctantly allowed Brown's attorneys to postpone their closing arguments until Monday morning. A frustrated Harding chose not to delay his closing argument and gave it that night. He rambled to the jury for about forty minutes as an embarrassed Andrew Hunter sat and listened.

He went over the testimony of witnesses and argued that Brown's claim that he should have been treated according to the rules of war was absurd.

The court then adjourned until 9:00 A.M. on Monday. As the court adjourned, John Brown, who had earlier claimed that he was too ill to be in court, rose off his cot and walked out of the courtroom with ease.

Day Five

On Sunday, Hiram Griswald and Samuel Chilton went over the notes of Lawson Botts and Thomas Green. They discovered that their predecessors were capable attorneys who had fought a good battle without much ammunition. The evidence against Brown was overwhelming. The prosecution had been successful in proving the facts they said they would prove. Like Botts and Green before them, Griswald and Chilton decided that their only option was to concentrate on the law, not the particular facts of the case. They would first argue that the court lacked jurisdiction. Second, as a backup, they would argue that while the evidence showed Brown was guilty of second-degree murder, it did not mean he was guilty of treason, insurrection, or first-degree murder.

On Monday morning, Griswald and Chilton made their closing arguments. The arguments of the two attorneys sounded much like their predecessors' opening statements.

Griswald and Chilton claimed that this Virginia court had no jurisdiction to hear the case. Since many of the crimes charged took place in a federal arsenal, only a federal court could try John Brown for those crimes. They also argued that the court did not have jurisdiction over the events that took place on the bridge. The bridge was over the Potomac River, the border between Maryland and Virginia, and the prosecution had failed to prove that it had jurisdiction in this area.

Regarding the charge of treason, they argued that common law required that the accused be a citizen of the state against which he is accused of committing treason. Since Brown was not a citizen of Virginia, he could not be convicted of committing treason against it.

They knew that Brown would be convicted of murder.

Suffering from wounds inflicted at Harpers Ferry, Brown spent most of the trial on a cot, even though doctors said his injuries were not serious.

People had been killed, and although Brown may not have personally fired a shot that killed anyone, he was the leader of the group and thus responsible for the actions of others. They did, however, hope that if they could show an absence of malice, Brown would be convicted only of second-degree murder. They relied on the testimony of most of the hostages and their claims that Brown had said that he did not desire bloodshed and had gone to lengths to protect them. They claimed that this showed the lack of planning in any killings.

Concerning insurrection, they argued that the fact that no slaves willingly joined Brown to help in his revolt proved that no insurrection had occurred. They also attempted to portray Brown's provisional government as an "imaginary government for a debating society."[8]

The attorneys for John Brown were successful in at least being able to make legal arguments that would allow a jury to acquit Brown of all offenses punishable by death. So, if the jury wanted to acquit Brown—declare him innocent of all charges—they were provided the legal excuses to do so. But Brown and his attorneys knew that this jury was not looking for any legal excuses to acquit; they were looking for a legal excuse to convict. The capable Andrew Hunter was about to provide them with all of the excuses they needed.

In all criminal cases, the prosecution has the last word. Hunter stood for his closing argument. Unlike Harding's rambling and confusing closing argument, Hunter was able to skillfully counter each of the points brought out by Griswald and Chilton.

Hunter countered the jurisdiction argument by citing a Virginia law specifically giving the court authority over crimes committed over the Potomac River. He agreed that the federal government had jurisdiction over the events that took place in the arsenal. This jurisdiction was not exclusive, however. That is, both Virginia and the federal government had jurisdiction since the arsenal lay within the borders of Virginia (concurrent jurisdiction). He also reminded the jurors that of the four murders that took place, each victim was shot outside the arsenal grounds.

Hunter then took up the question of treason. Brown's attorneys maintained that under Virginia law treason can only be committed by a citizen of the state in which the treason occurred. And neither Brown nor any of his followers, or recruited slaves, were citizens. Hunter again cited Virginia law to refute this point,

> Our Code defines who are citizens of Virginia, as all those white persons born in any other State of this Union who may become residents here. The evidence in this case shows, without a shadow of a question, that when this man came to Virginia and planted his feet on Harper's Ferry, he came there to reside and hold the place permanently.[9]

He went on to challenge the argument that Brown showed no malice in any of the murders. First-degree murder requires premeditation (malice). But first-degree murder can also be found when a murder is committed during the course of committing another felony (any serious crime). This situation is true even today. If a person goes into a store to commit a robbery (a felony) and ends up killing someone in the process, then he or she is guilty of first-degree murder. This is true even if the murder was not planned.

Hunter told the jury, "With regard to malice, the law was, that if the party perpetrating a felony, undesignedly takes life, it is a conclusive proof of malice."[10] Since John Brown committed murder while committing insurrection and treason, he was also guilty of murder in the first degree.

Hunter did not accept the idea that Brown's provisional government was merely a "debating society." He claimed that because Brown was not successful in his insurrection Brown was not free from responsibility for starting it. "The law says the prisoners are equally guilty, whether insurrection is made or not."[11]

Hunter concluded with the following reference to justice:

> Administer it according to your law—acquit the prisoner if you can—but if justice requires you by your verdict to take his life, stand by that column uprightly, but strongly, and let retributive justice, if he is guilty, send him before that maker who will settle the question forever and ever.[12]

Throughout the closing arguments, Brown laid back with his eyes closed. Hunter had taken apart the defense's arguments one at a time. It was now time for the jury to deliberate on a verdict. The court recessed while the jury retired to the deliberation room. Few people in the entire country doubted what the verdict would be.

chapter seven

THE VERDICT

VIRGINIA—As the jury considered its verdict, hundreds of people gathered outside the courthouse. The people of Virginia were about see "justice" for the crimes against the South. Reporters from all over the country wrote of the nervous tension that had gripped the South throughout the trial. That tension was about to come to a close.

The jury took only forty-five minutes to reach a verdict. Attorneys, spectators, and reporters swarmed back into the packed little courtroom. The people in the back of the room stretched and struggled to get a glimpse of John Brown. He stood seemingly unmoved by the events around him.

The clerk began to read the charges against John Brown and then asked, "Gentleman of the Jury, what say you, is the prisoner at the bar, John Brown, guilty or not guilty?" The foreman responded "guilty." The clerk inquired, "Guilty of treason, and conspiring and advising with slaves and others to rebel, and murder in the first degree?" The foreman simply answered "yes."[1]

The reporters from the North expected to hear loud applause from the Southern spectators, but as the verdict was read, the courtroom was silent. Chilton stood and asked the court to overturn, or reverse, the jury's verdict. He claimed that there were errors in the charges. Judge Parker said he would hear arguments about Chilton's motion the next day, but this was a mere legal formality. Brown's fate was sealed. The next step would be sentencing.

Sentencing

The next day John Brown and his attorneys entered the courtroom. Judge Parker overruled Chilton's motion to dismiss the case. The court then proceeded to sentencing. Brown, who was under the impression that he would be sentenced with the rest of his coconspirators who were still being tried, was surprised at the speed of the sentencing. The flustered Brown seemed to gather himself as he realized that these would be some of the last words he ever spoke. He rose from his cot and addressed not only the court but also the country with the following words:

> In the first place, I deny everything but what I have all along admitted: the design on my part to free slaves. . . . That was all I intended. I never did intend murder, or treason, or the destruction of property, or to excite or incite slaves to rebellion, or to make insurrection.[2]

After a moment, Brown continued:

I have stated from the first what was my intention, and what was not. I never had any design against the life of any person, nor any disposition to commit treason, or excite slaves to rebel, or make any general insurrection. I never encouraged any man to do so, but always discouraged any idea of that kind.[3]

Judge Parker sentenced John Brown to death by hanging. The sentence was to be carried out on December 2, 1859. Brown had one month to live.

chapter eight

THE CREATION OF A MARTYR

COURTHOUSE—No one in the country was surprised with the verdict or the sentence Judge Parker imposed. But this did not stop the Northern outcry over it and the Southern rejoice. By the time of sentencing, newspapers and politicians throughout the country had expressed their opinions about the trial and the sentence. The opinions were divided by North and South.

Although most Northern newspapers had, at first, sympathized with John Brown's cause, they later condemned him for the raid on Harpers Ferry. Editorials in *The New York Times* had been critical of those who supported the raid. They now criticized Judge Parker for refusing to grant postponements. They criticized the prosecution for playing on Southern fears of another slave rebellion. Abolitionist papers stopped just short of calling for an all-out war against Virginia and the rest of the South if Brown was to be hanged.

Southern newspapers

portrayed the trial as fair and agreed with the sentence imposed by Judge Parker. In the minds of Southerners, John Brown was still a criminal and, as the newspapers were quick to point out, a Northern criminal.

Brown was successful in what he had originally intended to accomplish with his raid on Harpers Ferry. In the end, it was not the South putting Brown on trial for attempting to free the slaves; it was Brown putting the South on trial for slavery. Brown now had one month to immortalize himself and to demonize the South.

Brown's True Intentions

Brown's speech at his sentencing was regarded by many poets and authors of the time as one the greatest speeches ever given. The American poet Ralph Waldo Emerson would later compare it to the Gettysburg Address. Much of the speech was in the spirit of Brown's intention to put the South on trial. Some of it, however, seemed in conflict with his actions and other statements. In his speech, Brown said that he never intended to excite slaves to rebel. Yet throughout the trial, and in his own statements, particularly his statement after being captured, he seemed to admit that rebellion was, in fact, his intention.

In a letter to Andrew Hunter, Brown attempted to explain this conflict. He wrote,

> When called in court to say whether I had anything further to urge, I was taken wholly by surprise, as I did not expect my sentence before the others. In a hurry of the moment I forgot much that I had intended to say.[1]

He explained that his statement to Governor Wise was accurate regarding his true intentions at Harpers Ferry, not the statement at sentencing. He did not directly say that he intended to start a slave rebellion, but he did state "that it was my object to place the slaves in a condition to defend their liberties."[2]

Governor Wise's Dilemma

Brown's attorneys filed motions appealing the conviction, but the court of appeals upheld Brown's conviction. Only one person—Governor Wise—could now save Brown from death.

Letters poured into the governor's office urging him to spare Brown's life. Some asked for humanitarian reasons; others asked because they feared that reaction in the North would lead to violence against the South.

John Brown was not the only person to recognize his potential as a martyr. Amos A. Lawrence, who had helped finance Brown in Kansas, warned Governor Wise, "From his blood would spring an army of martyrs, all eager to die in the cause of human liberty."[3] New York mayor Fernando Wood, a supporter of the South and friend of Governor Wise, wrote,

> Now, my friend, dare you do a bold thing, and 'temper justice with mercy'? Have you nerve enough to send Brown to the State Prison instead of hanging him?. . . . Circumstances create a sympathy for him even with the most ultra friends of the South.[4]

Some abolitionists secretly hoped that Brown *would* be

executed so that Northerners would flock to the abolitionist cause. Others hoped not so secretly for the same thing. The abolitionist preacher Henry Ward Beecher told his followers, "Let Virginia make him a martyr. . . . His soul was noble; his work miserable. But a cord and gibbet [a hangman's noose] would redeem all that, and round up Brown's failure with a heroic success."[5]

Governor Wise knew that Virginia was creating a martyr. But he felt that life in prison for Brown would do the same. In addition, Wise was a politician who had his eyes on the

Brown, arms bound with rope and sitting on his coffin, rides in a horse-drawn wagon to the site of his execution.

presidency. To change Brown's death sentence to a prison sentence would be political suicide. John Brown had to die.

John Brown's Last Days

From the time sentencing was imposed to the time of his execution, John Brown wrote to friends and supporters. Many of these letters were printed in northern newspapers. He did not ask to be saved but wrote to say good-bye and to urge the recipients of the letters to continue the fight against slavery. These letters demonstrate that Brown was well aware of his status as a martyr.

In a letter to his wife he wrote,

> I say here that the sacrifices you; and I have been called to make on behalf of the cause we love, the cause of God; and of humanity: do not seem to me as at all too great. . . . I feel quite determined to make the utmost possible out of a defeat.[6]

Because Brown realized that he was more valuable to "the cause" dead than alive, he urged others not to attempt to rescue him.

Despite Brown's unwillingness to be rescued, there were those who planned to do just that. One plan involved Brown's old Missouri comrades and German immigrants who intended to storm the jailhouse. Another desperate plot involved kidnapping Governor Wise and holding him hostage in order to exchange him for Brown. None of these plans really got off the ground. The security at Charleston was too heavy, and few wanted to finance such a risky attempt for a man who did not want to be rescued.

Brown clearly wanted to remain a strong symbol for the abolitionists. He did not want to show any fear of death or emotional weakness. Perhaps this is why he refused to see his wife until the day before his execution. Brown and his wife were reunited for four hours in his cell on December 1, 1859. Little is known about the visit, but we do know that Brown's wife had already lost three sons and was about to lose her husband.

In his last letter to his family, Brown wrote,

> I am waiting the hour of my public murder with great composure of mind and cheerfulness; feeling the strong assurance that in no other possible way could I be used to so much advantage to the cause of God and of Humanity. . . . John Brown writes his children to abhor, with undying hatred also, that sum of all villanies—slavery.[7]

The security surrounding Brown's execution was extensive. Governor Wise was convinced that troops were gathering in Ohio and Kansas to free Brown and invade Virginia. He convinced President Buchanan to send Colonel Robert E. Lee and hundreds of troops to guard Harpers Ferry. Days before the execution, Charleston was gripped in a state of fear. Numerous people, including four congressmen, were arrested on suspicion when they reached Charleston. But no invasion from the North was coming. All plots to rescue Brown had, by this time, been abandoned.

December 2, 1859, was a sunny, warm day in Charleston. As John Brown exited his cell for the last time, he saw an open wagon with a pine box containing an oak coffin. Brown sat himself on top of the pine box, and the wagon began to cross the large field to the gallows. Brown saw two lines of soldiers on each side of the wagon. Groups of curious citizens and newspaper reporters gathered outside the field. Only the military was allowed near the gallows.

At the scene were various people who would soon change history. They would play their part in the upcoming Civil War. Among those in attendance were Thomas J. Jackson, soon to be known as General "Stonewall" Jackson, one of the great Southern generals of the Civil War. Also present was a young actor and member of the militia, John Wilkes Booth. Booth would later assassinate President Abraham Lincoln.

John Brown climbed on top of the gallows without hesitation. All witnesses to the event would agree that Brown was true to his last letter to his family. He stood straight, tall, and composed. He shook the hands of the jailer and sheriff, who by all accounts treated Brown well throughout his jail time. Brown took off his hat, and the sheriff placed a white linen hood over his head. The jailer put the knotted rope around Brown's neck and guided him to the trap door. Then an unbearable delay took place while still-arriving troops took their positions around the gallows. The sheriff finally cut the rope holding the trap door.

In a letter to his wife, Thomas Jackson described the event as follows:

> Brown fell through about five inches, his knees falling on a level with the position occupied by his feet before the rope was cut. With the fall his arms, below the elbows, flew up horizontally, his hands clinched; and his arms gradually fell,

but by spasmodic motions. . . . Soon the wind blew his life-less body to and fro.[8]

Colonel J. T. L. Preston of the Virginia Military Academy approached the scaffold of the gallows and pro-claimed, "So perish all such enemies of Virginia! All such enemies of the Union! All foes of the human race!"[9]

John Brown was dead.

What Became of the Others

The other men who invaded Harpers Ferry with John Brown were also tried, convicted, and executed by the state of Virginia. Governor Wise remained governor of Virginia and was a strong supporter of the South leaving the Union. He

When Brown was sentenced to death by hanging, he was not upset. He realized his death would make him a martyr for the abolitionists.

lost a son in the Civil War. Lawson Botts served his home state of Virginia as a Confederate colonel. He was killed in the second battle of Bull Run. Thomas Green served alongside his associate, Botts, and survived the war. Andrew Hunter also survived the war but was financially ruined when Northern troops burned his house to the ground. Henry Hunter died of pneumonia as a private in the Confederate Army.

chapter nine

THE LEGACY OF JOHN BROWN

LEGACY—John Brown's most chilling and accurate prediction was about the country's future and it came on the day of his execution. Before he was led to the gallows, he handed one of his guards a note that read, "I, John Brown, am now quite certain that the crimes of this guilty land will never be purged away but with blood. I had, as I now think vainly, flattered myself that without very much bloodshed it might be done."[1]

Two years after Brown's execution the country plunged itself into the bloodiest war in its history—the Civil War. The clash between the North and the South ended after four years, and over six hundred thousand deaths.

In 1882, twenty-three years after John Brown's raid, abolitionist Frederick Douglass gave a speech at Harpers Ferry. He said, "John Brown began the war that ended American slavery, and made this a free republic."[2]

In 1865 John Brown's dream of a country without slavery finally came true when the Thirteenth Amendment to the Constitution was ratified.

Questions for Discussion

1. What, if anything, should John Brown's attorneys have done differently?

2. What, if any, mistakes did the prosecution make?

3. If you were Judge Parker, what, if anything, would you have done differently?

4. Did John Brown have a fair trial?

5. Do you think John Brown was guilty of insurrection? Treason? Murder?

6. Should John Brown have been tried in a federal court instead of a Virginia court?

7. Would a jury in the North have convicted John Brown?

8. Should Governor Wise have reduced John Brown's sentence of death to life in prison?

9. If Wise had reduced Brown's sentence, would this have changed Brown's status as a Northern martyr?

10. Did John Brown's raid on Harpers Ferry influence Southern resentment toward the North?

11. Did Brown's trial and execution influence Northern resentment toward the South?

12. Was John Brown's attempt to end slavery in the way he intended acceptable?

Chapter Notes

Chapter 1. A Nation Divided

1. Stephen B. Oates, *To Purge This Land with Blood* (New York: Harper & Row Publishers, 1970), p. 133.

Chapter 2. The Institution of Slavery

1. Steven B. Oates, *Stories of Great Crimes and Trials: Children of Darkness* (New York: McGraw-Hill Book Company, 1973), pp. 280–289.

2. Ibid., p. 228.

3. Frederick Douglass, *Life and Times of Frederick Douglass* (New York: Collier Books, 1962), p. 342.

Chapter 3. John Brown: The Man

1. Frederick Douglass, *Life and Times of Frederick Douglass* (New York: Collier Books, 1962), p. 340.

2. W. E. B. DuBois, *John Brown* (New York: International Publishers, 1974), p. 258.

3. Douglass, p. 339.

4. Stephen B. Oates, *To Purge This Land with Blood* (New York: Harper & Row Publishers, 1970), pp. 126–137.

5. Ibid.

6. Oswald Garrison Villard, *John Brown, 1800–1859: A Biography Fifty Years After* (Gloucester, Mass.: Peter Smith, 1965), pp. 245–246, 248.

Chapter 4. Harpers Ferry

1. F. B. Sanborn, *Life and Letters of John Brown* (Cedar Rapids, Iowa: Torch Press, 1910), pp. 562–571.

2. Ibid.

3. Ibid.

Chapter 5. The Trial Begins

1. Robert M. DeWitt, *The Life, Trial, and Execution of Captain John Brown* (New York: Robert M. DeWitt, 1859), p. 55. This is the closest thing to a true transcript of the trial available. In one form or another, this is the original source for most quotes from the trial.

2. Ibid., pp. 59–61.

3. Thomas J. Fleming, *Stories of Great Crimes and Trials: The Trial of John Brown* (New York: McGraw-Hill Book Company, 1973), p. 167.

4. DeWitt, p. 62.

5. Ibid.

6. Ibid., p. 64.

7. Richard Warch and Jonathan F. Fanton, *John Brown* (Englewood Cliffs, N.J.: Prentice Hall, Inc., 1973), p. 73.

8. DeWitt, p. 69.

Chapter 6. The Case for the Defense

1. Robert M. DeWitt, *The Life, Trial, and Execution of Captain John Brown* (New York: Robert M. DeWitt, 1859), p. 76.

2. James Redpath, *The Public Life of Captain John Brown* (Boston: Thayer and Eldridge, 1890), p. 64.

3. DeWitt, p. 77.

4. Ibid.

5. Ibid., p. 79.

6. Ibid., p. 83.

7. Jules Ables, *Man on Fire* (New York: The Macmillan Company, 1971), p. 329.

8. DeWitt, p. 92.

9. Ibid.

10. Ibid.

11. Ibid.

12. Ibid.

Chapter 7. The Verdict

1. Robert M. DeWitt, *The Life, Trial, and Execution of Captain John Brown* (New York: Robert M. DeWitt, 1859), p. 93.

2. Ibid., pp. 94–95.

3. Ibid.

Chapter 8. The Creation of a Martyr

1. Richard D. Webb, *The Life and Letters of Captain John Brown* (London: Smith Elder and Company, 1865), p. 43.

2. Ibid.

3. Allen Nevins, *The Emergence of Lincoln* (New York: Charles Scribner's Sons, 1950), p. 91.

4. Ibid.

5. Robert Penn Warren, *John Brown, The Making of a Martyr* (New York: Payson and Clarke, 1929), pp. 415–417.

6. Nevins, p. 96.

7. Louis Ruchames, *A John Brown Reader* (New York: Abeland-Schuman 1859), p. 87.

8. Thomas J. Fleming, *Stories of Great Crimes and Trials: The Trial of John Brown* (New York: McGraw-Hill Book Company, 1973), p. 180.

9. Nevins, p. 97.

Chapter 9. The Legacy of John Brown

1. F. B. Sanborn, *Life and Letters of John Brown* (Cedar Rapids, Iowa: Torch Press, 1910), p. 620.

2. W. E. B. DuBois, *John Brown* (New York, International Publishers, 1974), p. 265.

Glossary

abolitionist—An individual who wanted to end slavery in the United States.

American Colonization Society—The first organized abolitionist group in the United States.

arraignment—The first proceeding in the trial process, after an indictment is handed down. The indictment is read, bond may be set, and the case is scheduled for trial.

arsenal—A building in which military weapons and ammunition are stored.

bail/bond—A sum of money posted by a defendant to assure that he or she will appear at trial.

Bleeding Kansas—The name given to the violent and bloody events that took place while Kansas was applying for statehood. The violence took place between abolitionist and proslavery forces trying to determine whether Kansas would be a free or a slave state.

closing arguments—Arguments given by attorneys at the close of all of the evidence in a trial.

Free Soil Party—A political party formed in 1848 to stop the spread of slavery into the new United States territories.

free state—Any state that made slavery illegal.

Fugitive Slave Act—A federal law that made it illegal for anyone to help or hide a runaway slave; this included people in free states.

grand jury—A group of citizens who are empowered by law to hand down indictments.

guerrilla warfare—A military tactic by which a smaller force, quickly and by surprise, attacks a larger force and then flees before the larger force can counter attack.

indictment—A document handed down by a grand jury listing crimes that the grand jury found probable cause to exist. The defendant is then be tried on those charges.

insurrection—An uprising against an authority, usually a government.

jurisdiction—The matters that a particular court has power to hear.

Kansas-Nebraska Act—A federal law that allowed the people of those territories to vote to decide if they would be admitted to the Union as a free state or a slave state.

Liberty Party—A political party made up of abolitionists. The party's goal was to end slavery in the United States in its entirety.

malice—To do something with the intention of ill will.

martyr—Someone who dies for a cause.

militia—A body of citizens trained as a military force. It is called into action only when there is an emergency.

Missouri Compromise—A federal law enacted in 1818 making any state entering the Union north of the southern border of Missouri a free state and any state south of the border a slave state. Missouri was the exception to this law, because it was admitted as a slave state.

opening statement—Statements made by attorneys at the beginning of a trial. It is meant to give the jury a preview of the evidence it will hear.

preliminary hearing—The first formal step in the trial process. Charges against the defendant are announced and bond or bail is set. This process takes place before an indictment is announced.

probable cause—A standard of proof that must be shown to allow the prosecution to go forward to trial. At least some evidence to support the charges must be shown.

provisional government—A temporary government that is formed until an election can establish a permanent government.

subpoena—A court order requiring a witness to appear for trial.

treason—Betrayal of one's country or government.

Underground Railroad—A system of safe houses that helped runaway slaves travel to Canada, where they would be free.

voir dire—The process by which a jury is chosen.

Whig party—An early American political party that eventually evolved into the Republican party.

Further Reading

Barrett, Tracy. *Harpers Ferry: The Story of John Brown's Raid*. Brookfield, Conn.: Millbrook Press, Inc., 1993.

Browne, William F. *Two Kinds of Courage: Frederick Douglas and John Brown—a Look at Their Relationship*. New York: Spiritual Nerve, 1995.

Collins, James L. *John Brown and the Fight Against Slavery*. Brookfield, Conn.: Millbrook Press, Inc., 1991.

Cox, Clinton. *Fiery Vision: The Life and Death of John Brown*. New York: Scholastic, Inc., 1997.

Potter, Robert R. *John Brown: Militant Abolitionist*. Austin, Tex.: Raintree Steck-Vaughn Publishers, 1994.

Stein, R. Conrad. *John Brown's Raid on Harpers Ferry in American History*. Berkeley Heights, N.J.: Enslow Publishers, Inc., 1999.

Tackach, James. *The Trial of John Brown*. San Diego, Calif.: Lucent Books, 1998.

Internet Addresses

The National Park Service, Harpers Ferry National Historic Park

<http://www.nps.gov/hafe/home.htm>

John Brown Historical Association of Illinois

<http://www.cyberword.com/johnbrown>

Index